OCD
SAYINGS TO KEEP YOU SANE

REMINDERS, AFFIRMATIONS AND SLOGANS!

Obsessive Compulsive Disorder Anonymous

OCD: SAYINGS TO KEEP YOU SANE © 2013 All material in this book is, unless otherwise stated, the property of the author. Copyright and other intellectual property laws protect these materials. You may not, except with express written permission, distribute, or commercially exploit the content. Nor may you transmit it or store it in any other website or other form of electronic retrieval system. Reproduction or retransmission of the materials, in whole or in part, in any manner, without the prior written consent of the copyright holder, is a violation of copyright law. Users may not distribute such copies to others, whether or not in electronic form, whether or not for a charge or other consideration, without prior written consent of the copyright holder of the materials. Some of the material contained in this publication may be found elsewhere in electronic form. Any electronic representations of this work are included within this copyright and all rights are thus reserved. Any redistribution or reproduction of part or all of the contents of this work in any form is prohibited with the following exceptions:

(1) You may print or download to a local hard disk extracts which must not exceed one page in length for the purpose of creating published reviews, critiques, analyses, instructional material or reports which will be disseminated in a public forum such as a newspaper, magazine, blog, online magazine or other electronic publication. In all such cases you must include: The original copyright notice as it appears here and, reference to the original source of the material and where it can be obtained.

(2) You may share website links related to this material by using any of the share icons at the bottom of each page (Google Mail, Blogger, Twitter, Facebook, GoogleBuzz); Providing a back-link or the URL of the content you wish to disseminate; and, or quoting extracts from the electronic material of website with attribution to **www.thesolutioncenter.com**

Contact information for questions regarding this copyright notice or for requests for permission to reproduce or distribute materials available through this protected material may be directed to The Solution Center, P.O. Box 6654, Grand Rapids, MI 49516

Library of Congress Cataloging in Publication Data
Komor, Christian R., 1959-

OCD: Sayings to Keep You Sane!

    1. Stress 2. Anxiety 3. Self-Help

ISBN-13: 978-1484038673

ISBN-10: 1484038673

Publisher: The Solution Center
                  P.O. Box 6025
                  Grand Rapids, Michigan 49516
                  www.thesolutioncenter.com

DEDICATION

To all OCD sufferers who struggle daily with this arduous and painful disorder. You have our respect and admiration for your courage, strength and hope – whether today you are just "hanging on" or making great strides forward. May you find the love, support and courage you need for your journey from the darkness of OCD and the comfort of friends who will share that journey of recovery with you!

CONTENTS

COPYRIGHT NOTICE..2

DEDICATION..4

A (TOOTHLESS) WOLF IN SHEEPS CLOTHING...6

REMINDERS, AFFIRMATIONS AND SLOGANS...11

THE FAIRYTALES' END..54

THE TOOTHLESS WOLF IN SHEEPS CLOTHING

I saw the overhead road sign from several miles away. Used to send helpful messages to drivers in case of high winds or other hazardous conditions it currently displayed no message – at least not to anyone else. For me it spelled out certain doom!

My Obsessive Compulsive Disorder had for some reason chosen this harmless road sign as "significant" – associating going under the sign with horrible and immediate illness and death. My type of OCD has always been most associated with thresholds, changes in conditions, turning something on or off, getting out of bed, standing up from a chair, beginning or ending something, doorways, cracks in the pavement, steps, walls, even rocks or trees I had to walk between on a pathway in the woods. Of course, it is impossible to negotiate life without encountering thresholds, or beginnings and endings. Life is filled with this stuff.

This particular type of overhead sign, however, had always plagued me. Once, early on in my experience with OCD, I drove six hours back to repeat going under some stupid road sign in Northern Michigan which my brain had chosen to associate with doom! A few years older and wiser in the ways of OCD as I approached this new nemesis I was ready to do battle. No longer a neophyte in the OCD Wars I knew the secret to defeating my enemy was to <u>unmask</u> him – to pull the proverbial sheep's clothing off and see the OCD for what it was – a genetic problem with my brain wiring. To do this I was armed with a pocket full of sayings – simple reminders that the OCD was just an error message in my brain – not real and not a threat. Approaching at 65mph I chose my specific weapon swiftly:

"Ask yourself; Would anyone <u>without</u> OCD see this as a threat?"

Well, of course not, I thought. Otherwise there would be hoards of people circling this 30 foot high road sign like ancient druids worshiping an oblisque. Instead all the other cars were just driving underneath without a second thought. So I grabbed my slogan and charged ahead and guess what? Nothing horrible happened! For the billionth time OCD had been lying to me. And without my reminder/slogan to help me <u>detach</u> from the OCD and see it as just an illusion – just a wolf in sheep's clothing – I would have gotten sucker in again and lost another little bit of my life.

Ranked as the 10th most disabling medical disorder by the World Health Organization, Obsessive Compulsive Disorder affects millions of adults and children around the world. OCD is a genetically-determined neuro-immune problem resulting in ritual behaviors in an attempt to reduce terrifying cognitions.

To date the only reliable form of treatment for OCD requires exposing oneself to feared situations and refusing to perform the anxiety-reducing rituals this stimulates. This requires immense courage and diligent awareness of the *unreal nature of obsessional thoughts* - akin to convincing oneself a seizure or drug-induced hallucination is not real! Statistics suggest that even with carefully targeted medication and cognitive-behavioral therapy, a substantial percentage of patients do not receive substantial relief from symptoms. It becomes important, then, to develop technologies for long-term self-care and lifestyle management. One such tool is the use of daily meditations, reminders, sayings, and slogans. These reminders can help us to separate ourselves from obsessional thoughts and learn to disbelieve them! Like a refreshing slash of cold water, or a friendly tap on the shoulder they remind us that thoughts are just thoughts and need not control our reactions. And meditating on slogans or sayings can also have other benefits:

Meditations and affirmations can also act as reminders of skills that one is developing through the exposure and response prevention behavior therapy process.

They can reduce feelings of isolation – reminding us that we are not alone in our fight against obsessions and compulsions.

They can assist us in generating hope that recovery from OCD is possible and remind us of active steps we can take to better our situation.

They can assist us in developing and embracing new perspectives on living without the illusory protection of anxiety reducing rituals.

They can assist in keeping a steady pace in the recovery process – a process that is won by continual, gradual progress resulting in very real change in the brain.

But most of all slogans, sayings and reminders can assist us in separating ourselves from the lies and deceptions fed to us by our OCD mind. They help us to take a step back and examine our obsessional thoughts in the cold light of day – punching holes in the lies of OCD. With their help we can drive a wedge between the obsessions and our REAI and beliefs.

Most critical is that we **stop believing the OCD!** And so, contained within this small-but-powerful book are dozens of the most helpful sayings that have emerged through the thousands of interviews we have conducted. Many have similar themes, but sometimes OCDers need just the right wording to turn off the part of our brain where our thoughts get stuck. Choose sayings and carry them in a wallet or purse for ready use when OCD strikes. Post them up in key locations around the house. Say them to yourself quietly as you confront an obsession and struggle to refuse a compulsion.

This book is copyrighted, but the sayings contained within are gifts for you to use on your journey of recovery from OCD. Use them freely and where and when you need them. May your journey of recovery be blessed with friends and fortune.

*The **OCD** Serenity Prayer: "God grant me the ability to control things I cannot control, the courage to change the things I can, and who cares about the difference!"*

*The **Real** Serenity Prayer: "God grant me the serenity to accept the things I cannot change, the courage to change the things I can, and the wisdom to know the difference."*

REMINDERS, AFFIRMATIONS AND SLOGANS

"And the day came when the risk it took to remain tight inside the bud was more painful than the risk it took to blossom." – Anais Nin

You can't stop bad things with your rituals. Life is inherently risky.

Live on the Universe's plan - which is always simple.

*Too much compulsive control leads to being **out of control**.*

If you fear suffering you are already suffering.

OCD is a guide to learning about self-ownership!

See that the thoughts are just OCD. Refuse to cooperate. Ride the wave of anxiety. Make NO DEALS with it. Do it because loved ones need you and the world needs you!

Take the hit as a gift!

Refuse to do one ritual, then USE that to empower yourself! Look back on it and say, "If I didn't have to do that then I don't have to do this either." Soon breaking OCD's rules feels GOOD and you want to do it again and again!

Health is not everything. **Feeling good** *is everything.*

OCD relies on our human skill of associating things together – but takes it way too far!

You can't put out fire with gasoline.

Don't stop a minute before a miracle.

What will be, will be……and so it has always been right?

OCD is an illusion and it has had too much of your life already.

Find ways to soothe yourself! People with OCD are have deep anxiety and must learn to self-soothe!

Anxiety is the fuel that drives OCD. Take steps to reduce your anxiety and you will reduce your OCD.

For many of us OCD is linked to mental and emotional constriction and self-denial. OCD tends to "pull back" when you try to let go and have fun. Know it's okay to enjoy what you are doing - that God wants us to enjoy the gifts of life!

*Remember, OCD or no OCD, life **does** come to an end someday. You might as well play!*

OCD is being stuck! Move, wiggle around it, get unstuck, detaching, let go.

You CAN'T go wrong when you say no to the OCD! It will ALWAYS FEEL WRONG but it will not BE WRONG! Rather it will be RIGHT and in your best interests!

*The "cognitive" part – detaching and seeing the OCD for what it is (just OCD) – does not have to be done AT THAT TIME! It can take place after the event - so just **keep going**.*

Are you any more "certain" about this [than] other times?

Have you ever NOT performed a ritual "required" by the OCD? Sure you have. Did you survive? Sure you did. So that means this current ritual is a lie also!

Ask, "Would anyone without OCD have to go back and do this?"

Other stuff will be happening ALSO (panic, guilt, self-identity), BUT that makes no difference. Deal with the OCD as separate – it is NEVER okay!

OCD tends to fuse a thought with an action. If you do X behavior or think X thought something terrible will happen. Challenge those associations – they are errors!

*When you break out of OCD life is exhilarating! Isn't it amazing to be free to do as you wish! Don't you want to feel that **always**?*

OCD can try to get at you with a spoken name or word, an image, a feeling, or even just a felt-sense. Just see what it throws at you next with detached interest and don't react.

Trust God's plan not OCDs plan!

Ask, "Is this OCD? Do I do OCD? No."

to Keep You Sane

...e what the OCD is going to come up
...he "flavor of the day") to get you to
...will. Whatever it is – don't do it!

If what OCD told you was true everyone would be doing it – or there would be a lot of dead people!

You can't jump from the first step to the second landing. You take a stand and then start to feel better and one step at a time you get more freedom.

Ride the waves of anxiety after refusing the OCD – it will pass. OCD hits ARE the opportunity and FEAR **is the medicine!**

If you think about it – the chemicals that our own brains make are the ONLY ones that will fit US exactly. Change your behavior, feel the fear, and the **fear will act as medicine** to change your brain!

Having a brain soaked in OCD we tend to feel like we are doing everything wrong. That feeling of "something is wrong" trails us around. Remember that and you can shake it! Your fine!

OCD connects with loss of self. You must commit to self-ownership!!!! Often that begins with saying, "No".

"If thine eye offends thee pluck it out"

Take a bold action and you may actually **shift out** *of the OCD part of your brain that wants to stifle you and hold you back.*

Take time to settle, center and see the OCD clearly for what it is. To see through the OCD pause and look at this lie and then all the past lies – see through the illusion.

If you have to use something to get through a tough OCD moment, the idea is to give the OCD as little reinforcement as possible and leave a little risk.

Trust God - these are Just Thoughts. Then know that you are NOT in danger – at least not in the way you feel. Then remember everyone dies and it's okay. This OCD fear is of imaginary death.

Don't focus on the thought as this will just turn on the OCD part of your brain. Feel the anxiety – love yourself – cry if it's there – feel the tight chest or knot in your stomach - get back in your body!

Instead of performing the ritual do something nice for yourself.

the AM – get out in the sun and walk around other people.

The OCD gets you to look at things the wrong way. Ask, "Do other people have to do _____ to be okay?"

Ask, "Do I want to live forever appeasing the OCD like this - because that's where this is headed?"

Notice the OCD is taking away the very things you do the rituals to protect – self-care, exercise, relationships, pleasure, hiking, etc. OCD will kill you if it gets the chance! Don't let it!!

Notice how the OCD does not let you rest – keeps you in a constant state of fearful agitation!

Notice obsessional thoughts are basically hallucinations. We believe our thoughts have validity but they do NOT!

Remember there will ALWAYS be beginnings and endings and "significant" situations. The OCD ALWAYS tells you this situation is critical! It lies!

If you find yourself in a deal with the OCD don't try and work it out. Realize the whole thing is wrong! you got tricked. There IS no deal – you never promised to deal with the OCD. Just STOP!

17 | OCD: Sayings to Keep You Sane

Mornings can be difficult because our cortisol levels are higher and we do not feel safe. Our anxiety goes up and then our OCD is triggered. Remember this pattern and be extra kind and soothing to yourself in the morning!

Do not start the day running from fear. Stand your ground. Breath, relax and unmask the OCD.

We often need to risk deliberately – like doing a paper drop with our feared word written on it. Perhaps moving and soothing are what you need in

OCD: Sayings to Keep You Sane

Say "SO WHAT!" Which means being just a little lighter about death..... Bonzai!

NEVER follow a "Maybe....?" — is not Real

Thoughts are just thoughts! They are not promises, agreements, predictions, foreshadowing's, wishes, making a reservation, casting a shadow, or anything else – no matter how it seems or feels.

For many it is refusing to accept the inevitability of physical death that gives the OCD its power. Say to the OCD "Go ahead and kill me OCD if that is the way things work, but hey why don't others have to do these rituals?"

[handwritten: Ask yourself — Is it True?]
[handwritten: Thought is not Real!!]

Imagine (remember) how easy life can be without OCD. How effortless and smooth sailing. Don't you want to feel like that again?

We often get SO caught up in the schemes (obsessions and responses) that we forget that it is ALL OCD. Say, "NO DEALS".

If you break out of the OCD it will break you out of any horrible brain-locked dissociative depression you might be stuck in.

Love chases out fear. Wake up your self-care and your want-to.

The goal is just turning off the OCD part of your brain – deactivating it.

Don't try to avoid bad thoughts as if they will do something to you. Instead just go on with your life and accept that bad thoughts will happen. They are just hallucinations.

It's giving the thought importance that causes problems – and then all you do to avoid it like redoing, erasing, trying to get the thought right, thinking good thoughts in advance, etc., etc.

21 | OCD: Sayings to Keep You Sane

The KEY is these are JUST THOUGHTS (not reality) – like in the movie "A Beautiful Mind".

our thoughts are not Reality

All associations to place and activity, beginning and ending are irrelevant.

Let go and let God.

Sometimes the "weather" will be smooth and sometimes rough. Just do the right thing and see it all as thoughts hallucinations regardless.

We often don't relax because the OCD tells us that will mean that we "don't care" and thus deserve doom! It's not true!

It is very helpful to be out and about with other people. What we can gain from others is perspective on the OCD.

Sometimes a bigger OCD ritual (and the pain of doing it) can lead you to fighting harder through the following smaller rituals. Use what you have to fight!

Keep your head out of the "OCD mode". Shut off that area of the brain and when it's shut off work to keep it shut off! Migrated that OCD-Free way of thinking to your entire day.

Use stuck places as opportunities by only giving the OCD part of what it wants – then see that you didn't have to give it anything.

Remind yourself how much better it feels to not give in to OCD.

First things first.

OCD recovery is like a diet. When we act on a compulsion (to eat or perform a ritual) we are practicing avoidance of (anxiety). The result is for the anxiety to grow stronger (or our stomach to grow bigger!).

Remember that OCD is a disorder in the brain, not of our character! We all have within us a "good dog" and a "bad dog". The one we feed is the one that becomes the strongest. Don't feed the OCD dog and it will grow weaker.

To beat OCD is to choose to live with uncertainty.

Good and bad things will happen in life and, yes, we all die eventually. The only choice for those of us with OCD is whether to spend the life we have as a slave to OCD - or as a free, spontaneous person.

See that your OCD can potentially connect you to a greater spirituality and self-discovery.

Trust God...and tie your camel! Know the difference between what you can do something about and what it is best to let go of.

Surrender to the anxiety feeling. Feel it and it will get tired of bothering you.

Progress not perfection.

*Recovery is about trust. The antidote for the holding-on-fear-of-everything-syndrome is **really trusting** (God, the Universe, Higher Power).*

Notice how you do something and then think "Oh, I did that without OCD. Maybe..." and then the OCD starts up with "what if's". Instead just keep going and don't get into that loop!

Don't do the behavior AND trigger your relaxation response (explore ways of doing this).

Get anxiety under control before OCD happens!

Thoughts do not make reality and feelings aren't facts.

OCD is the opposite of free-will. Giving in to "shoulds" leads to OCD.

Admitting powerlessness over OCD is the 1st Step.

Obsessions live in the future and the past. Keep your mind in the Now!

Validation and affirmation from outside are needed and important. Use books, media, whatever fits.

What works to break you out of OCD's spell one time may not the next. You may have to alternate, or change up interventions.

Avoid H.A.L.T. (Hungry, Angry, Lonely, Tired)

Find a neutral zone, or safe place you can re-center in and use it.

Remember, OCD is the anxiety part of the pie and has nothing to do with real illness or real death or real disasters.

OCD does not cause illness – it IS your illness. You have a disease and it's OCD. You also have a body and it has both health and ill health. OCD does not protect you from illness. There is no connection.

If you give in to the OCD it ruins the time you do have to live your life.

You can NEVER do ANY "good" OCD behaviors.

Half measures avail us nothing.

It cannot be that ALL compulsions are real can it?

*Say, "It's a brain disorder. It's a false message coming from my brain" AND **Believe it**!*

*Do not **resist** OCD. Develop a "spectator" approach. Say "It's not me it's the OCD." Call it what it really is - an obsessive symptom. It's not a real feeling, or need.*

*OCD is just a medical symptom. It's too strong to resist unless you know what it really is. It doesn't go away **because** it is medical.*

ENJOY breaking the OCD barriers deliberately!

Remember some of us get manic-like when we come out from under the OCD-depression and start to feel our spontaneous energy again. At such times - go slow and stay connected.

Say "I can do it in 15 minutes if I still need to." Then move on. Do something else instead.

Others around you do not have to do these rituals to be ok so you don't either!

You didn't always have to do these rituals so why should you now?

Don't wait to feel like the desire is gone to not do the behavior! Your behavior will never change if you wait for the urge to change first.

Change your behavior so that the feeling/urge will change.

One day at a time.

Temporary discomfort is the price of freedom. Keep going forward.

OCD does not protect against bad results. Self-care and relaxation does.

There is no quick easy solution. Take the long-term road of not giving in versus the quick fix that OCD offers.

Escaping risk leads to greater (real) risk. There is often less danger in the things we fear than in the things we desire.

Refuse to act on an obsession and it will die of inaction.

You can't have your symptoms and behaviors and have your life.

Paradoxes are the major reason for getting stuck in OCD. OCD recovery is measured by living according to your values.

Change occurs when one loves what one is not when one becomes what one is not.

OCD will isolate you. You have to choose between OCD and a happy life and relationships.

You cannot control what thoughts pop into your head. You can control what happens next.

If you ever doubt what to do – ask what the average person would do.

If nothing changes, nothing changes.

If we keep one foot in tomorrow and one foot in yesterday we step over today.

Never trust OCD. It always lies.

Things turn out for the best to people who play the cards they got.

Pain may be inevitable, but misery is not.

If you want to make God laugh, make plans.

The life tools you pay most dearly for are the ones you don't use.

If you must suffer, suffer for a purpose.

*Just because you **think it** doesn't mean you did it (or want to do it). Actions are actions and thoughts are thoughts.*

It only looks risky. Only risks will bring rewards.

Easy does it – But do it!

If it's not broken, don't fix it.

Keep it simple.

OCD is not fair and life is not fair.

You cannot perfect your symptoms.

Worry does not empty tomorrow of its sorrow. It empties today of its strength! - Corrie TenBoom (Nazi concentration camp survivor)

Where there is life there is hope.

Treat OCD as an opponent in your pursuit of happiness and fight against it daily.

To beat OCD is to choose live with uncertainty – without compulsions and obsessions to try and control the uncertainty.

Progress always has detours.

Good and bad things will happen in life and, yes, you will die eventually. The only choice for those of us with OCD is whether to spend the life you have a slave to OCD or not.

OCD is just a medical symptom. It's too strong to resist unless you know what it really is. It doesn't go away **because** *it is medical.*

People with OCD gain perspective from being around others. We see that on the OCD. Other stuff from relationships is nice, but perspective is what we need.

Logic and reason don't make the OCD drives go away, but it does help us decide whether not to listen to them.

You still can't put out fire with gasoline.

Remember that OCD is a disorder in the brain not in character.

See that your OCD can potentially connect you to a greater spirituality and provide an opening for self-discovery.

Surrender to the anxiety feeling. See it as medicine! Feel it, and it will get tired of bothering you.

Recovery is about trust. The antidote for the holding-on-fear-of-everything-syndrome is really trusting (God, the Universe, your Higher Power).

Decelerate to disinhibit. We can get going so fast in our compulsions. Slow down in order to get back to your spontaneity.

If you give in to the OCD it ruins the time you do have to live your life.

Reorient to (1) self-care and (2) finding your center by detaching.

Say, "It's a brain disorder. It's a false message coming from my brain". Do not resist. Develop a "spectator" approach. Say "It's not me it's the OCD." Call it what it really is - an obsessive symptom. It's not a real feeling, or need.

ENJOY breaking the OCD barriers deliberately!

Remember some of us get manic-like when we come out from under the OCD- depression and start to feel our spontaneous energy again. At such times - go slow and stay connected.

Say "I can do it in 15 minutes if I still need to." Then move on. Do something else instead.

Others around you do not have to do these rituals to be ok so you don't either!

You didn't always have to do these rituals so why should you now?

Realize if you give in it will tighten the "lock" and make it stronger. To loosen the lock, don't give in. If you don't feed it and it will get weaker.

Don't wait to feel like the desire is gone to not do the behavior! Your behavior will never change if you wait for the urge to change first.

You can't have your symptoms and behaviors and have your life.

Change your behavior so that the feeling/urge will change.

Temporary discomfort is the price of freedom. Keep going forward.

OCD does not protect against bad results. Self-care and relaxation does.

There is no quick easy solution. Take the long-term road of not giving in versus the quick fix that OCD offers.

Escaping risk leads to greater (real) risk. There is often less danger in the things we fear than in the things we desire.

Refuse to act on an obsession and it will die of inaction.

Paradoxes are the major reason for getting stuck in OCD.

OCD = "What if?"

OCD recovery is measured by living according to your values not your obsessions.

Change occurs when one loves what one is not when one becomes what one is not.

Our discomfort with an uncertain existence leads to perfectionist control and that leads to rigidity and depression of spontaneity. We want to control what cannot be controlled and play god in that way.

In dealing with obsessions (1) shift your focus inward and then (2) RELAX.

The KEY is bare attention. Being fully present to THIS MOMENT takes you out of the OCD part of your brain. Even combining that with light OCD is not so bad.

We spend so much time dancing with the OCD and telling ourselves it DOES matter. To turn it off, or down, you have to tell yourself – so what it doesn't matter it's just an illusion.

See through the OCD... pause and look at this lie and then all the past lies.. see through the illusion.

If you have to use something to get through - the idea is to give the OCD as little reinforcement as possible and leave a little risk.

Go for the positive – replace the obsessional thought with a positive ("I trust life not OCD")

It's easier to get in the mode where you stay out of the OCD mind. The hard thing is when the voice of OCD is really loud and you are getting stuck left and right.

Moving and soothing are often what OCDers need in the morning on waking – get out in the sun and walk around other people.

Notice how the OCD does not let you rest – keeps you in a constant state of fearful agitation!

You try to avoid bad thoughts as if they will do something to you. Instead just go on with your life and accept that bad thoughts will happen. They are just hallucinations.

It's giving the thought importance that causes problems – and then all you do to avoid it like redoing, erasing, trying to get the thought right, thinking good thoughts in advance, etc., etc.

"Beginnings" and "endings" are irrelevant.

Ultimately you have to get MAD and say "I don't care. I am not letting this have my life." And just refuse to do it.

Why worry about what you cannot change!

Give the OCD "requirements" to GOD.

OCD is not how the world works. You don't control outcomes this way. Let go. Be aware of and don't give in to OCD "dares". Say "No Dares!"

Work to see it for OCD what it is – develop mindfulness and detachment from thoughts

Feel the fear rather than avoiding it!

Celebrate small decreases in OC. It builds rapidly in a positive (or negative) direction. As you go less effort produces more change.

If you give in to an obsession at least admit it won this time around – and thus admit that it is just a brain glitch and not "real".

Part of the OC is "don't feel good about my life or something bad may happen". It's obsession!

Don't obsess (e.g. when waking up) or "stare" at yourself.

Sometimes the "weather" will be smooth and sometimes rough. Just do the right thing and see it all as thoughts hallucinations regardless.

Relax and let go even if the OCD is telling you that will mean you are reckless and "don't care". It's not true!

You STILL *can't put out fire with gasoline.*

THE FAIRYTALES' HAPPY ENDING

You do not need to leave your room.
Remain sitting at your table and listen.
Do not even listen, simply wait.
Do not even wait, be quite still and solitary.
The world will freely offer itself to you to be unmasked.
It has no choice, it will roll in ecstasy at your feet.
    - Franz Kafka

Long before Walt Disney was a gleam in Mickey & Minnie's eyes, fairytales were warning children of the potential dangers they might encounter in the "woods" of life. Like a master storyteller OCD weaves for us who are forced to listen stories of horror and disaster. Disasters avoidable only through arcane magical rituals performed over and over and over and over again. And like children asking for a story to be read a second time, no matter how many times the OCD has told us it's latest horror story we are still captivated – mesmerized and held in its spell. And no matter how many times we have ventured out only to find OCD's stories were fairytale fabrications, gossamer illusions with no substance – we still somehow believe.

It's time we broke the spell of OCD - stopped following its bizarre and arcane rituals! The slogans, sayings, affirmations and reminders in this book are designed to do just that. Using them as a shield and a sword you will cut a path through the illusions of OCD and remember what is real.

As part of our recovery from OCD many of us challenge ourselves to set exposure and response prevention goals. In doing so we write new and happier endings to the fairytale horrors that OCD concocts. We confront OCD's fairytale rituals through proactive behavior change – Exposure and Response Prevention.

As essential as these behavior change goals can be to achieve, we should not mistake them for more than intermediate steps between the agony of obsessions and compulsions and **the life that we are seeking**. Beyond the pain of OCD, and the hard work of behavior therapy, there must lie some reward – something we can look forward to! A pot of gold, as it were, at the end of the rainbow. Let's spend a minute or two and talk about what life can be like without obsessions and compulsions.

We are living at this very moment in the Garden of Eden. Surrounding us is a world of unbelievable beauty, peace, and utter fulfillment created, many of us believe, by a loving God. We can see and experience the hand of grace in the sunlight glistening off the water, the wind drifting through the trees, the rains nurturing the earth. Even better, we have an amazing variety of fellow creatures with whom to share this with. Truly our world is a garden of delights waiting to be experienced. Each moment we are alive on this earth holds the potential for joy, fulfillment and serenity. Life is inherently designed to be a wonderful experience. Just the basics of being alive (eating, breathing, working, sleeping) can be incredible *experiences*. The pot of gold at the end of our recovery rainbow, it turns out, has been right here under our noses all the time. The problem is, wrapped up in our obsessions and compulsions, we have been unable to open it. Our compulsions block us from entering into a spontaneous, alive and rewarding experience of living. Cognitive and behavior therapies are simply the tools we use to achieve our ultimate goal of aliveness and health being!

It is important to understand that the power of spontaneous being is within us form birth and does not disappear. Rather it is covered over by compulsive behavior generated by misfiring neurons from our brains. Healthy being is the polar opposite of obsessive-compulsive behavior. Paradoxically, those of us with OCD are in an excellent position to experience and appreciate healthy being. Without the struggle of obsessive-compulsive behavior we are less likely to appreciate the sweetness and joy of healthy being.

We have all had times when we connected with this state of healthy being - On a vacation when we let our guard down and truly relaxed or after challenging ourselves successfully with a piece of exposure and response prevention work. When approaching life from the perspective of healthy being, the inherent perfection and spiritual harmony in the natural world can be experienced. In the state of *being* a powerful feeling of aliveness and connection to our bodies is experienced. The environment seems to come alive and we may be thrilled with the wonderful elements of the natural world. A sense of

...se and letting go in our relationships is developed so that ...rs are accepted rather than controlled, or treated as objects ...ependency. A sense of destiny and an acceptance of the

flow of life is also likely to be present along with a deep awareness of one's Higher Power.

Healthy being leads us to:
- Make decisions and choices out of self-ownership rather than an externalized ideal of how things "should" look.
- Accept all experiences in life as holding potential for personal growth and enhancement.
- Carry with us an inner resolve to relax fully in all situations – even when it seems we should be tense and upset.
- Focus our attention on the present moment rather than on our fears and projections regarding the past or future.
- Listen to our spontaneous inner voice as opposed to the voice of our obsessions.
- Be committed to transparency and congruency in relationships so that we interact with others as our true self rather than a façade.
- Enjoy the process as much or more than attaining goals.
- Balance our time between self-care and self-wear.
- Be patient and persevering in our approach to life and our own growth process.

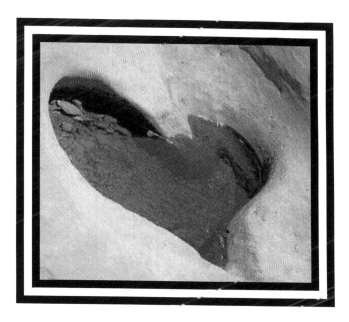

Words and ideas cannot really capture the *feeling* of being. There is no way to *know* what it is really like to be in touch with your spontaneous self except by *direct experience*. You will know what it is like to *be* when you have been there and not a minute before that! Most people recognize the spontaneous sense of aliveness that is characteristic of being and slowly begin to learn the individual psychological path they must follow to return to it again and again. Just as we develop the ability to walk, not from being told how or "figuring it out," but by actual trial and error, so do we gradually develop an inner *experience* of what it is like to *be*. Gradually the awareness of the being side of living grows stronger and life without beingness begins to look flat and unfulfilling.

The increased ability to "just be" also means that the healing compulsive person is less likely to be acting out through rituals and fear-driven behaviors to avoid feelings and especially anxiety. When healing from obsessive-compulsive behavior, we begin to pay increasing amounts of attention to

what we feel inside. Instead of compulsive rituals or accomplishing things, we spend more time feeling feelings and sharing them. At first these feelings may seem like weird aliens within, but gradually we learn to listen to them even when we don't know for sure where they will lead. We develop a sense of trust in our destiny and an ability to take up the thread of our feelings knowing that the total fabric will show itself eventually.

What can help provide the courage to make the journey from doing to being is the awareness that even a lifetime of material success and good work *pales when compared to even a few hours of true beingness.* When we are brave enough to face down shoulds, we make a contribution to the world that is as real as it is difficult to measure. When you think of the people who have most influenced your life or those you have felt most loved by, it is likely you will find that they had a

strong quality of being about them. When we are into beingness, wonderful things begin to happen to us and around us and other people benefit either directly or indirectly.

As part of an ability to live in the moment, we learn the importance of the five senses. In healing we discover that it is those experiences that involve the *senses* that are most enjoyable and that are most real. We become able to be still long enough to appreciate the smell of a spring afternoon, to feel the warm sun in the morning on the way to work, to enjoy the cool water we drink, to make love and take pleasure in the sensuality of the experience, to feel our bodies and sense the messages they have. We begin to see the intrinsic God-given value in what we sense. Our experience becomes a teacher as well as a guide.

Coming home to our self is a wonderful feeling. In the midst of obsessive-compulsive behavior we may even have

stopped believing that *we* still exist. It sounds funny, but many recovering obsessive-compulsives will say that they had even forgotten what it *felt* like to be their true self! Recovering from obsessive-compulsive behavior means finding our identity as people again. We recover the person we were meant to be.

As someone who has been traveling this road I can assure you that you *are* still the wonderful human being that you started out to be. When you begin to recover your sense of really *being*, you will know this is true. In those moments, hours, or days in your life when you have been able to move beyond obsessive-compulsive behavior and feel really at peace you may have experienced a sense of serenity and wholeness, a sense of somehow being different. Instead of feeling separate from the world and other people through attempts to control, such moments bring a sense of flowing — of being part of life in a deeply spiritual and fulfilling way. When we are deep into obsessive-compulsive behavior, it helps to remember that sense of serenity is always there *inside* waiting for us to shift perspectives and behaviors enough so that it can *come out*. The end of the recovery rainbow is right here, right now. It's time we talk about it.

SEVERAL BLANK PAGES FOLLOW WHERE YOU CAN WRITE YOUR OWN SAYINGS OR AFFIRMATIONS!

OCD: Sayings to Keep You Sane

OCD: Sayings to Keep You Sane

OCD: Sayings to Keep You Sane

57 | OCD: Sayings to Keep You Sane

Made in the USA
San Bernardino, CA
15 September 2017